The Luminous Mysteries

AN ILLUSTRATED ROSARY BOOK FOR KIDS AND THEIR FAMILIES

THE ILLUMINATED ROSARY
Revised Edition

TEXT BY JERRY WINDLEY-DAOUST
ORIGINAL CONCEPT BY MARK DAOUST

For an introduction to praying the rosary with this book, see page 92.

The Canticle of Mary (Magnificat)

My soul proclaims the greatness of the Lord;
    my spirit rejoices in God my Savior
    for he has looked with favor on his lowly servant.
From this day all generations will call me blessed;
    the Almighty has done great things for me
    and holy is his name.
He has mercy on those who fear him
    in every generation.
He has shown the strength of his arm,
    and has scattered the proud in their conceit.
He has cast down the mighty from their thrones,
    and has lifted up the lowly.
He has filled the hungry with good things,
    and the rich he has sent away empty.
He has come to the help of his servant Israel
    for he has remembered his promise of mercy,
    the promise he made to our fathers,
    to Abraham and his children forever.

In the name of the Father,
  and of the Son, and of the Holy Spirit.
Amen.

I believe
  in God, the Father almighty,
  Creator of heaven and earth,
and in Jesus Christ,
  his only Son, our Lord,
  who was conceived by the Holy Spirit,
born of the Virgin Mary,
  suffered under Pontius Pilate,
was crucified, died and was buried;
he descended into hell;
  on the third day he rose again from the dead;
he ascended into heaven,
  and is seated at the right hand
  of God the Father almighty;
from there he will come to judge
  the living and the dead.

I believe in the Holy Spirit,
  the holy catholic Church,
  the communion of saints,
  the forgiveness of sins,
  the resurrection of the body,
  and life everlasting.

Amen.

Our Father
  who art in heaven,
    hallowed be thy name.
Thy kingdom come.
Thy will be done on earth,
    as it is in heaven.

Give us this day our daily bread,
and forgive us our trespasses,
as we forgive those
    who trespass against us,
and lead us not into temptation,
    but deliver us from evil.

Amen.

FOR FAITH

Hail, Mary, full of grace, the Lord is with thee.
Blessed art thou among women,
and blessed is the fruit of thy womb, Jesus.
Holy Mary, Mother of God, pray for us sinners,
now and at the hour of our death. *Amen.*

FOR HOPE

Hail, Mary, full of grace, the Lord is with thee.
Blessed art thou among women,
and blessed is the fruit of thy womb, Jesus.
Holy Mary, Mother of God, pray for us sinners,
now and at the hour of our death. *Amen.*

FOR CHARITY

Hail, Mary, full of grace, the Lord is with thee.
Blessed art thou among women,
and blessed is the fruit of thy womb, Jesus.
Holy Mary, Mother of God, pray for us sinners,
now and at the hour of our death. *Amen.*

Glory be to the Father,
and to the Son, and to the Holy Spirit;
as it was in the beginning, is now, and ever shall be
world without end. *Amen.*

The Baptism of Christ in the Jordan

In those days, people from all of Judea
traveled into the wilderness
to be baptized by a man named John.

"Turn away from sin,
for the Kingdom of heaven has come near,"
John told them. "Someone is coming
who is more powerful than me.
I have baptized you with water;
but he will baptize you with the Holy Spirit."

Jesus also came to be baptized by John;
and as he came up out of the water,
he saw the heavens torn apart
and the Spirit descending like a dove on him.

And a voice came from heaven:
"You are my Son, the Beloved;
with you I am well pleased."

INTENTIONS

Our Father
  who art in heaven,
    hallowed be thy name.
Thy kingdom come.
Thy will be done on earth,
    as it is in heaven.

Give us this day our daily bread,
and forgive us our trespasses,
as we forgive those
    who trespass against us,
and lead us not into temptation,
    but deliver us from evil.

Amen.

Hail, Mary, full of grace, the Lord is with thee.
   Blessed art thou among women,
      and blessed is the fruit of thy womb, Jesus.

Holy Mary, Mother of God, pray for us sinners,
   now and at the hour of our death. *Amen.*

Hail, Mary, full of grace, the Lord is with thee.
Blessed art thou among women,
and blessed is the fruit of thy womb, Jesus.

Holy Mary, Mother of God, pray for us sinners,
now and at the hour of our death. *Amen.*

The Baptism of Christ in the Jordan

Hail, Mary, full of grace, the Lord is with thee.
  Blessed art thou among women,
    and blessed is the fruit of thy womb, Jesus.

Holy Mary, Mother of God, pray for us sinners,
  now and at the hour of our death. *Amen.*

Hail, Mary, full of grace, the Lord is with thee.
  Blessed art thou among women,
    and blessed is the fruit of thy womb, Jesus.

Holy Mary, Mother of God, pray for us sinners,
  now and at the hour of our death. *Amen.*

Hail, Mary, full of grace, the Lord is with thee.
Blessed art thou among women,
and blessed is the fruit of thy womb, Jesus.

Holy Mary, Mother of God, pray for us sinners,
now and at the hour of our death. *Amen.*

Hail, Mary, full of grace, the Lord is with thee.
Blessed art thou among women,
and blessed is the fruit of thy womb, Jesus.

Holy Mary, Mother of God, pray for us sinners,
now and at the hour of our death. *Amen.*

Hail, Mary, full of grace, the Lord is with thee.
Blessed art thou among women,
and blessed is the fruit of thy womb, Jesus.

Holy Mary, Mother of God, pray for us sinners,
now and at the hour of our death. *Amen.*

Hail, Mary, full of grace, the Lord is with thee.
  Blessed art thou among women,
    and blessed is the fruit of thy womb, Jesus.

Holy Mary, Mother of God, pray for us sinners,
  now and at the hour of our death. *Amen.*

Hail, Mary, full of grace, the Lord is with thee.
Blessed art thou among women,
and blessed is the fruit of thy womb, Jesus.

Holy Mary, Mother of God, pray for us sinners,
now and at the hour of our death. *Amen.*

Hail, Mary, full of grace, the Lord is with thee.
Blessed art thou among women,
and blessed is the fruit of thy womb, Jesus.

Holy Mary, Mother of God, pray for us sinners,
now and at the hour of our death. *Amen.*

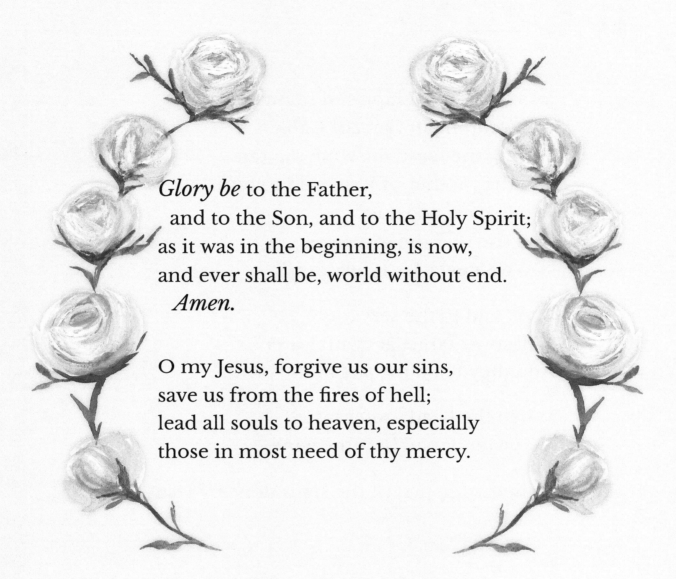

Glory be to the Father,
  and to the Son, and to the Holy Spirit;
as it was in the beginning, is now,
and ever shall be, world without end.
  Amen.

O my Jesus, forgive us our sins,
save us from the fires of hell;
lead all souls to heaven, especially
those in most need of thy mercy.

The Wedding Feast at Cana

Jesus and his disciples were invited
to a wedding in Cana of Galilee.
During the feast, the wine ran out,
and the mother of Jesus said to him,
"They have no wine."
And she told the servants,
"Do whatever Jesus tells you."

Jesus said to the servants,
"Fill some large jars with water."
And they filled the jars to the brim.

When the head waiter tasted
the water, it had become wine.

This was the first of the signs done by Jesus.

INTENTIONS

Our Father
who art in heaven,
hallowed be thy name.
Thy kingdom come.
Thy will be done on earth,
as it is in heaven.

Give us this day our daily bread,
and forgive us our trespasses,
as we forgive those
who trespass against us,
and lead us not into temptation,
but deliver us from evil.

Amen.

Hail, Mary, full of grace, the Lord is with thee.
 Blessed art thou among women,
  and blessed is the fruit of thy womb, Jesus.

Holy Mary, Mother of God, pray for us sinners,
 now and at the hour of our death. *Amen.*

Hail, Mary, full of grace, the Lord is with thee.
　Blessed art thou among women,
　　and blessed is the fruit of thy womb, Jesus.

Holy Mary, Mother of God, pray for us sinners,
　now and at the hour of our death. *Amen.*

The Wedding Feast at Cana

Hail, Mary, full of grace, the Lord is with thee.
Blessed art thou among women,
and blessed is the fruit of thy womb, Jesus.

Holy Mary, Mother of God, pray for us sinners,
now and at the hour of our death. *Amen.*

Hail, Mary, full of grace, the Lord is with thee.
   Blessed art thou among women,
      and blessed is the fruit of thy womb, Jesus.

Holy Mary, Mother of God, pray for us sinners,
     now and at the hour of our death. *Amen.*

Hail, Mary, full of grace, the Lord is with thee.
Blessed art thou among women,
and blessed is the fruit of thy womb, Jesus.

Holy Mary, Mother of God, pray for us sinners,
now and at the hour of our death. *Amen.*

Hail, Mary, full of grace, the Lord is with thee.
Blessed art thou among women,
and blessed is the fruit of thy womb, Jesus.

Holy Mary, Mother of God, pray for us sinners,
now and at the hour of our death. *Amen.*

Hail, Mary, full of grace, the Lord is with thee.
  Blessed art thou among women,
    and blessed is the fruit of thy womb, Jesus.

Holy Mary, Mother of God, pray for us sinners,
  now and at the hour of our death. *Amen.*

Hail, Mary, full of grace, the Lord is with thee.
Blessed art thou among women,
and blessed is the fruit of thy womb, Jesus.

Holy Mary, Mother of God, pray for us sinners,
now and at the hour of our death. *Amen.*

The Wedding Feast at Cana

Hail, Mary, full of grace, the Lord is with thee.
   Blessed art thou among women,
      and blessed is the fruit of thy womb, Jesus.

Holy Mary, Mother of God, pray for us sinners,
   now and at the hour of our death.   *Amen.*

Hail, Mary, full of grace, the Lord is with thee.
Blessed art thou among women,
and blessed is the fruit of thy womb, Jesus.

Holy Mary, Mother of God, pray for us sinners,
now and at the hour of our death. *Amen.*

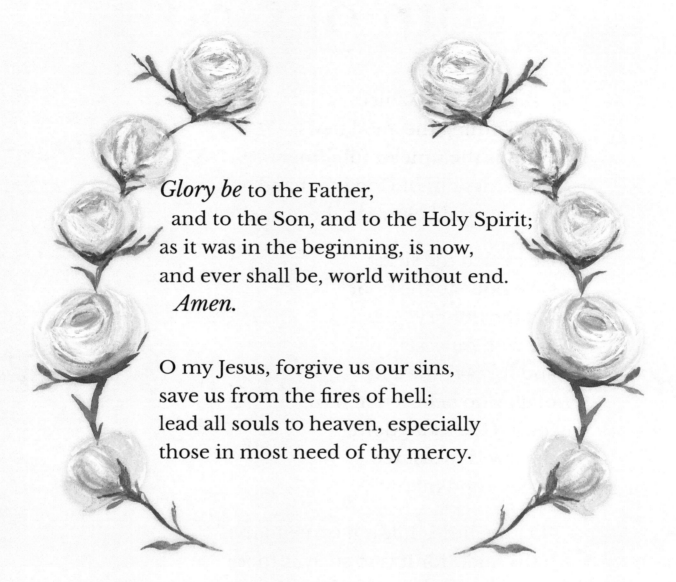

Glory be to the Father,
  and to the Son, and to the Holy Spirit;
as it was in the beginning, is now,
and ever shall be, world without end.
  Amen.

O my Jesus, forgive us our sins,
save us from the fires of hell;
lead all souls to heaven, especially
those in most need of thy mercy.

Jesus Proclaims the Kingdom of God

Jesus came to Galilee
proclaiming the good news:
"This is the time of fulfillment.
The kingdom of God is at hand.
Repent, and believe in the gospel."

He healed the sick,
gave hope to the poor,
fed the hungry,
ate with outcasts,
and forgave the sins
of all who believed in him;
for in God's kingdom,
the law is measured
by love and mercy.

"Let the little children come to me,"
Jesus said, "for it is to such as these
that the kingdom of God belongs."

INTENTIONS

Our Father

who art in heaven,
hallowed be thy name.
Thy kingdom come.
Thy will be done on earth,
as it is in heaven.

Give us this day our daily bread,
and forgive us our trespasses,
as we forgive those
who trespass against us,
and lead us not into temptation,
but deliver us from evil.

Amen.

Hail, Mary, full of grace, the Lord is with thee.
Blessed art thou among women,
and blessed is the fruit of thy womb, Jesus.

Holy Mary, Mother of God, pray for us sinners,
now and at the hour of our death. *Amen.*

Hail, Mary, full of grace, the Lord is with thee.
  Blessed art thou among women,
    and blessed is the fruit of thy womb, Jesus.

Holy Mary, Mother of God, pray for us sinners,
  now and at the hour of our death. *Amen.*

Hail, Mary, full of grace, the Lord is with thee.
  Blessed art thou among women,
    and blessed is the fruit of thy womb, Jesus.

Holy Mary, Mother of God, pray for us sinners,
  now and at the hour of our death. *Amen.*

Hail, Mary, full of grace, the Lord is with thee.
  Blessed art thou among women,
    and blessed is the fruit of thy womb, Jesus.

Holy Mary, Mother of God, pray for us sinners,
  now and at the hour of our death. *Amen.*

Hail, Mary, full of grace, the Lord is with thee.
  Blessed art thou among women,
    and blessed is the fruit of thy womb, Jesus.

  Holy Mary, Mother of God, pray for us sinners,
    now and at the hour of our death. *Amen.*

Hail, Mary, full of grace, the Lord is with thee.
Blessed art thou among women,
and blessed is the fruit of thy womb, Jesus.

Holy Mary, Mother of God, pray for us sinners,
now and at the hour of our death. *Amen.*

Hail, Mary, full of grace, the Lord is with thee.
Blessed art thou among women,
and blessed is the fruit of thy womb, Jesus.

Holy Mary, Mother of God, pray for us sinners,
now and at the hour of our death. *Amen.*

Hail, Mary, full of grace, the Lord is with thee.
  Blessed art thou among women,
    and blessed is the fruit of thy womb, Jesus.

Holy Mary, Mother of God, pray for us sinners,
  now and at the hour of our death. *Amen.*

Hail, Mary, full of grace, the Lord is with thee.
Blessed art thou among women,
and blessed is the fruit of thy womb, Jesus.

Holy Mary, Mother of God, pray for us sinners,
now and at the hour of our death. *Amen.*

Hail, Mary, full of grace, the Lord is with thee.
  Blessed art thou among women,
    and blessed is the fruit of thy womb, Jesus.

Holy Mary, Mother of God, pray for us sinners,
  now and at the hour of our death. *Amen.*

Glory be to the Father,
   and to the Son, and to the Holy Spirit;
as it was in the beginning, is now,
and ever shall be, world without end.
   Amen.

O my Jesus, forgive us our sins,
save us from the fires of hell;
lead all souls to heaven, especially
those in most need of thy mercy.

The Transfiguration

Jesus took Peter and James and John
up a high mountain. And there,
he was transfigured before them:
his face shone like the sun,
and his clothes became dazzling white.
The prophets Moses and Elijah appeared,
talking with Jesus.

A bright cloud came over them,
and from the cloud a voice said,
"This is my Son, the Beloved;
with him I am well pleased; listen to him!"

The disciples fell to the ground,
overcome by fear.

But Jesus came and touched them, saying,
"Get up and do not be afraid."
And when they looked up,
they saw no one except Jesus.

INTENTIONS

Our Father
  who art in heaven,
    hallowed be thy name.
Thy kingdom come.
Thy will be done on earth,
    as it is in heaven.

Give us this day our daily bread,
and forgive us our trespasses,
as we forgive those
    who trespass against us,
and lead us not into temptation,
    but deliver us from evil.

Amen.

The Transfiguration

Hail, Mary, full of grace, the Lord is with thee.
Blessed art thou among women,
and blessed is the fruit of thy womb, Jesus.

Holy Mary, Mother of God, pray for us sinners,
now and at the hour of our death. *Amen.*

Hail, Mary, full of grace, the Lord is with thee.
Blessed art thou among women,
and blessed is the fruit of thy womb, Jesus.

Holy Mary, Mother of God, pray for us sinners,
now and at the hour of our death. *Amen.*

The Transfiguration

Hail, Mary, full of grace, the Lord is with thee.
   Blessed art thou among women,
      and blessed is the fruit of thy womb, Jesus.

Holy Mary, Mother of God, pray for us sinners,
   now and at the hour of our death. *Amen.*

Hail, Mary, full of grace, the Lord is with thee.
  Blessed art thou among women,
    and blessed is the fruit of thy womb, Jesus.

Holy Mary, Mother of God, pray for us sinners,
  now and at the hour of our death. *Amen.*

The Transfiguration

Hail, Mary, full of grace, the Lord is with thee.
Blessed art thou among women,
and blessed is the fruit of thy womb, Jesus.

Holy Mary, Mother of God, pray for us sinners,
now and at the hour of our death. *Amen.*

Hail, Mary, full of grace, the Lord is with thee.
  Blessed art thou among women,
    and blessed is the fruit of thy womb, Jesus.

Holy Mary, Mother of God, pray for us sinners,
  now and at the hour of our death. *Amen.*

The Transfiguration

Hail, Mary, full of grace, the Lord is with thee.
  Blessed art thou among women,
    and blessed is the fruit of thy womb, Jesus.

Holy Mary, Mother of God, pray for us sinners,
  now and at the hour of our death. *Amen.*

Hail, Mary, full of grace, the Lord is with thee.
Blessed art thou among women,
and blessed is the fruit of thy womb, Jesus.

Holy Mary, Mother of God, pray for us sinners,
now and at the hour of our death. *Amen.*

The Transfiguration

Hail, Mary, full of grace, the Lord is with thee.
Blessed art thou among women,
and blessed is the fruit of thy womb, Jesus.

Holy Mary, Mother of God, pray for us sinners,
now and at the hour of our death. *Amen.*

Hail, Mary, full of grace, the Lord is with thee.
  Blessed art thou among women,
    and blessed is the fruit of thy womb, Jesus.

Holy Mary, Mother of God, pray for us sinners,
  now and at the hour of our death. *Amen.*

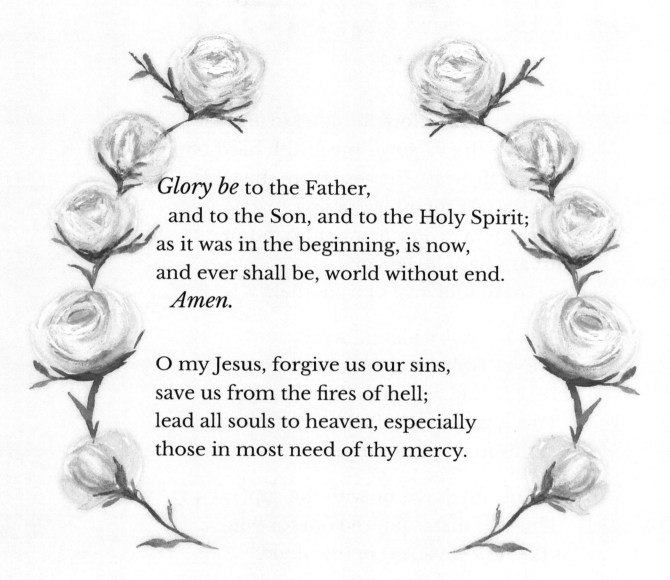

Glory be to the Father,
  and to the Son, and to the Holy Spirit;
as it was in the beginning, is now,
and ever shall be, world without end.
  Amen.

O my Jesus, forgive us our sins,
save us from the fires of hell;
lead all souls to heaven, especially
those in most need of thy mercy.

The Institution of the Eucharist

On the night before he suffered and died,
Jesus ate the Passover meal with his disciples.
During the meal, he rose from the table
and washed their feet, saying,
"I am giving you a new commandment:
Just as I have loved you,
so you should love one another."

Then he took a loaf of bread,
gave his Father thanks and praise,
broke it, and gave it to them, saying,
"This is my body, which is given for you.
Do this in remembrance of me."

And he did the same with the cup, saying,
"This cup that is poured out for you
is the new covenant in my blood.
It will be shed for you and for all
so that sins may be forgiven."

INTENTIONS

Our Father

who art in heaven,
    hallowed be thy name.
Thy kingdom come.
Thy will be done on earth,
    as it is in heaven.

Give us this day our daily bread,
and forgive us our trespasses,
as we forgive those
    who trespass against us,
and lead us not into temptation,
    but deliver us from evil.

Amen.

Hail, Mary, full of grace, the Lord is with thee.
  Blessed art thou among women,
    and blessed is the fruit of thy womb, Jesus.

Holy Mary, Mother of God, pray for us sinners,
  now and at the hour of our death. *Amen.*

Hail, Mary, full of grace, the Lord is with thee.
  Blessed art thou among women,
    and blessed is the fruit of thy womb, Jesus.

Holy Mary, Mother of God, pray for us sinners,
  now and at the hour of our death. *Amen.*

Hail, Mary, full of grace, the Lord is with thee.
Blessed art thou among women,
and blessed is the fruit of thy womb, Jesus.

Holy Mary, Mother of God, pray for us sinners,
now and at the hour of our death. *Amen.*

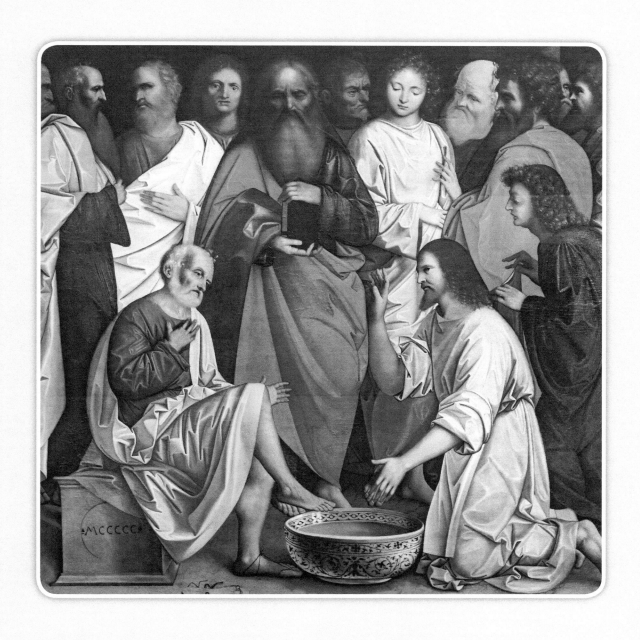

Hail, Mary, full of grace, the Lord is with thee.
  Blessed art thou among women,
    and blessed is the fruit of thy womb, Jesus.

Holy Mary, Mother of God, pray for us sinners,
  now and at the hour of our death. *Amen.*

Hail, Mary, **full of grace, the Lord is with thee.**
Blessed art thou among women,
and blessed is the fruit of thy womb, Jesus.

Holy Mary, Mother of God, pray for us sinners,
now and at the hour of our death. *Amen.*

Hail, Mary, full of grace, the Lord is with thee.
Blessed art thou among women,
and blessed is the fruit of thy womb, Jesus.

Holy Mary, Mother of God, pray for us sinners,
now and at the hour of our death. *Amen.*

The Institution of the Eucharist

Hail, Mary, full of grace, the Lord is with thee.
Blessed art thou among women,
and blessed is the fruit of thy womb, Jesus.

Holy Mary, Mother of God, pray for us sinners,
now and at the hour of our death. *Amen.*

Hail, Mary, full of grace, the Lord is with thee.
Blessed art thou among women,
and blessed is the fruit of thy womb, Jesus.

Holy Mary, Mother of God, pray for us sinners,
now and at the hour of our death. *Amen.*

Hail, Mary, full of grace, the Lord is with thee.
  Blessed art thou among women,
    and blessed is the fruit of thy womb, Jesus.

Holy Mary, Mother of God, pray for us sinners,
  now and at the hour of our death. *Amen.*

Hail, Mary, full of grace, the Lord is with thee.
Blessed art thou among women,
and blessed is the fruit of thy womb, Jesus.

Holy Mary, Mother of God, pray for us sinners,
now and at the hour of our death. *Amen.*

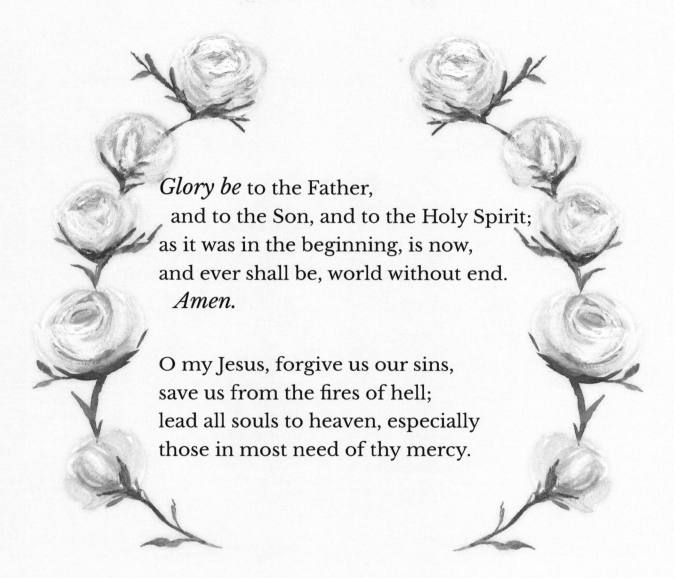

Glory be to the Father,
   and to the Son, and to the Holy Spirit;
as it was in the beginning, is now,
and ever shall be, world without end.
   Amen.

O my Jesus, forgive us our sins,
save us from the fires of hell;
lead all souls to heaven, especially
those in most need of thy mercy.

Hail, holy Queen,
Mother of Mercy:
our life, our sweetness and our hope.
To thee do we cry,
poor banished children of Eve;
To thee do we send up our sighs,
mourning and weeping in this valley of tears.
Turn then, most gracious advocate,
thine eyes of mercy toward us;
and after this our exile,
show unto us the blessed fruit of thy womb, Jesus.
O clement, O loving,
O sweet Virgin Mary.

V. Pray for us, O holy Mother of God.

R. That we may be made worthy of the
    promises of Christ.

In the name of the Father, and of the Son,
and of the Holy Spirit. *Amen*.

Art Credits

Cover: Andrei N. Mironov, *Marriage in Cana*, 2017. Licensed under CC BY-SA 4.0. Artist website: artmiro.ru

Title page, 23, 39, 55, 71, 87, back cover: Jessica Connelly, *Luminous Mysteries Rose Wreath*, 2018. All rights reserved. Used with permission. Artist website: https://telos.design

Title page: Unknown artist, *The Last Supper*. Licensed from Adobe Stock.

2–3: Gian Domenico Facchina, *Magnifcat*, 1895–1907. Photo by Fr. Lawrence Lew, O.P. Used with permission.

5: Bartolomé Esteban Murillo, *Christ the Good Shepherd*, 1660.

7: Jen Norton, *Hail Mary*, 2013. © Jen Norton. Used with permission. Artist website: jennortonartstudio.com

THE BAPTISM OF CHRIST IN THE JORDAN

8–9: Antoine Coypel, *The Baptism of Christ*, 1690.

10–11: Bonifaci Ferrer, *Baptism of Christ*, ca. 1400. Photography by Joanbanjo. Licensed under CC BY-SA 3.0.

12–13: Francesco Granacci, *Saint John the Baptist Bearing Witness*, 1506–1507.

14: Francesco Francia, *Baptism of Christ*, 1490. Photography by José Luiz Bernardes Ribeiro. Licensed under CC BY-SA 3.0.

15: Joachim Patinir, *Baptism of Christ*, 1510–1512.

16: Nicolas Poussin, *Saint John Baptizing in the River Jordan*, 1630s.

17: Karoly Marko, *Baptism of Jesus Christ*, 1860.

18: Mural in Skačkovce Monastery, Macedonia. Photography by Rašo. Licensed under CC BY-SA 3.0.

19: Dave Zelenka, *Baptism of Christ*, Wikimedia. Licensed under CC BY-SA 3.0. Artist website: www.lampofthebody.com

20: Peter Paul Rubens. *The Baptism of Christ*, 1605.

21: Master of the Saint Bartholomew Altarpiece, *The Baptism of Christ*, 1485–1500.

22: Daniel Bonnell, *The Baptism of the Christ*, 1999. All rights reserved. Used with permission.

Artist website: bonnellart.com

THE WEDDING AT CANA

24–25: John August Swanson, *The Wedding Feast*, 1996. © John August Swanson, All rights reserved. Used with permission. Artist website: www.johnaugustswanson.com

26–27: Andrei N. Mironov, *Marriage in Cana*, 2017. Licensed under CC BY-SA 4.0. Artist website: artmiro.ru

28: Daniel Mitsui, *Wedding at Cana*, 2014. All rights reserved. Used with permission. Artist website: danielmitsui.com

29: Philippe Grall, *The Wedding at Cana*, 2014. Property of Atelier Saint-Andre (Lausanne, Switzerland). All rights reserved. Used with permission. Artist website: atelier-st-andre.net

30–31: Paolo Veronese, *The Wedding at Cana*, 1563.

32: Juan de Flandes, The Marriage Feast at Cana, 1500–1504.

33: Maerten de Voos, *Marriage at Cana*, 1597. Photography by Joaquim Alves Gaspar. Licensed under CC BY-SA 4.0.

34: Johann Georg Platzer, *Marriage at Cana*, 1757.

35: Winifred Knights, *The Marriage at Cana*, 1923.

36: George Walsh, detail of stained glass window depicting second Mystery of Light, 2005. Photography by Andreas F. Borchert. Licensed under CC BY-SA 3.0.

37: Julius Schnorr von Carolsfeld, *The Wedding Feast at Cana*, 1819.

38: Unknown, *Wedding at Cana*. Licensed from Adobe Stock.

JESUS PROCLAIMS THE KINGDOM OF GOD

40–41: James Tissot, *Jerusalem, Jerusalem*, ca. 1886–1904.

42–43: Fritz von Uhde, *Suffer the Little Children to Come Unto Me*, 1884.

44: Pierre Mignard, *Christ and the Woman of Samaria*, 1681.

45: Jan Brueghel the Younger and Peter Paul Rubens, *Christ in the House of Martha and Mary*, 1628.

46: Bradi Barth, *Zacchaeus*. Copyright © HERBRONNEN vzw; all rights reserved. Used with permission. Artist website: bradi-barth.org

47: Jeanine Crowe, *I Fear No Evil for Thou Art with Me*, 1995. © Jeanine Crowe. Used with permission.

48: Duccio di Buoninsegna, *The Raising of Lazarus*, 1310–1311.

49: E.F. Mohn after G.C. von Max, *Jairus's Daughter*, date unknown (19th century). Photography courtesy Wellcome Collection. Licensed under CC BY 4.0.

50: Unknown artist, mural of the Good Samaritan. Licensed from Adobe Stock.

51: Vincent Van Gogh, *The Sower*, 1888.

52–53: James B. Janknegt, *2 Sons*, 2002. Used with permission. Artist website: bcartfarm.com

54: Sister Patricia Reed, RSCJ, *The Multiplication of the Loaves and Fishes*, ca. 2000. All rights reserved. Used with permission.

THE TRANSFIGURATION

56–57: Julia Stankova, *Transfiguration of Christ*, 2015. All rights reserved. Used with permission. Artist website: juliastankova.com

58–59: George Walsh, *The Transfiguration*, 2005. Photography by Andreas F. Borchert. Licensed under CC BY-SA 3.0.

60: James Tissot, *The Transfiguration*, 1886–1894.

61: Peter Paul Rubens, *The Transfiguration of Christ*, 1605.

62: Unknown artist, Transfiguration icon.

63: Pietro Perugino, *Transfiguration*, 1496–1500.

64: Master of the University Altar, *The Transfiguration of Christ*, 1500.

65: Fra Angelico, *Transfiguration*, 1442.

66: Andrei N. Mironov, *Transfiguration*, 2018. Licensed under CC BY-SA 4.0. Artist website: artmiro.ru

67: Unknown artist, mosaic of the Transfiguration in the Church of the Transfiguration, Israel. Photography by by Itamar Grinberg. Licensed under CC BY-SA 2.0.

68: Unknown Artist, *The Transfiguration of Christ*, Second half of 15th century.

69: Unknown Artist, *The Transfiguration of Our*

Lord in St. Leon Armenian Cathedral (Burbank), 2010.

70: Raphael, *The Transfiguration*, 1516–1520. Photography by Alves Gaspar. Licensed under CC BY-SA 4.0.

THE INSTITUTION OF THE EUCHARIST

72–73: Dr. Jose Miguel Fuenzalida-Comas, *Pencil Sketch of Jesus Christ*, 2004. Licensed under CC BY-SA 4.0.

74–75: James B. Janknegt, *Bread of Life*, 2014. All rights reserved. Used with permission. Artist website: bcartfarm.com

76: Leonardo da Vinci, *The Last Supper*, 1495–1498.

77: Antoni Estruch, *Last Supper*, 1898–1910. Licensed under CC BY-SA 3.0.

78: Unknown artist, fresco of Jesus washing the disciples' feet. Licensed from Adobe Stock.

79: Giovanni Agostino da Lodi, *Christ Washing the Disciples' Feet*, 1470.

80: Andrei N. Mironov, *Last Supper*, 2009. Licensed under CC BY-SA 4.0. Artist website: artmiro.ru

81: Jan Erasmus Quellinus, *The Last Supper*, ca. 1712. Licensed from Adobe Stock.

82: Unknown, lithograph of the Last Supper, late 19th century. Licensed from Adobe Stock.

83: Unknown, *The Last Supper*. Licensed from Adobe Stock.

84: Henryk Siemiradzki, *Last Supper*, 1876.

85: Unknown artist, mosaic of the institution of the Eucharist at the Last Supper in Medjugorje, Bosnia and Herzegovina. Licensed from Adobe Stock.

86: Daniele Crespi, *The Last Supper*, 1624–1625.

88: Unknown artist, *Ethiopian Icon XIX-XX*, early 18th century. Photography by Miguel Galles. Licensed under CC BY-SA 4.0.

Back cover: Jeanine Crowe, *I Fear No Evil for Thou Art with Me*, 1995. © Jeanine Crowe. Used with permission.

How to Pray the Rosary with This Book

WELCOME to THE ILLUMINATED ROSARY, a way of praying the rosary more meditatively with the help of sacred art. THE ILLUMINATED ROSARY was first developed for families with young children, but has proven popular with young and old alike.

Using THE ILLUMINATED ROSARY is simple:

- The *full text* of every prayer is printed in order, so that young readers might learn to pray the rosary without distraction.

- Each mystery is introduced with a brief, *child-friendly reading* loosely based on the Scriptures. In the rosary, a mystery is an episode in the life of Christ or Mary that unfolds God's plan of salvation. After reading about each mystery, you will be prompted to state the *intentions* for which you are praying.

- The *sacred art* on every spread is meant to aid prayerful meditation. As you pray each decade, remember the words of Pope Paul VI: "By its nature the recitation of the Rosary calls for a quiet rhythm and a lingering pace, helping the individual to meditate on the mysteries of the Lord's life..." (Pope Paul VI, Marialis Cultus #47).

- The roses around the text of each Hail Mary serve as *rosary beads*, helping kids keep track of where they are in the decade.

Here are some practical suggestions for praying THE ILLUMINATED ROSARY with children:

- *Keep it short* at first, saying one decade of the rosary in a single sitting. *Try praying antiphonally*: one group or person says the first half of each prayer, and the other group or person says the second half.

- Optionally, *ask your family for intentions* for each decade. For whom or for what do you wish to offer the prayers of the decade?

- After you are finished praying, *ask your children what thoughts or feelings* they had as they meditated on each mystery. Which artwork "spoke" to them most? How might the Holy Spirit have been speaking to them through their meditation?

You may find some of the artwork in these pages not to your personal taste. That is natural; but to get the most out of your meditation, try viewing these images sympathetically. Let the vision of the artist challenge you: Why would the artist paint the mystery as he or she did? What does it reveal to the artist and others who have appreciated it? However you use THE ILLUMINATED ROSARY, may praying with it lead you closer to the heart of Jesus through the heart of his mother; and may your own heart be filled with awe, reverence, and wonder.

The Joyful Mysteries *The Luminous Mysteries* *The Sorrowful Mysteries* *The Glorious Mysteries*

Dedicated to the memory of Norman G. Daoust.

Nihil obstat:
Rev. Timothy Hall, *Censor librorum*

Imprimatur:
†Most Rev. John M. Quinn, Bishop of Winona
May 13, 2015

The imprimatur is an official declaration that a book or pamphlet is free of doctrinal or moral error. No implication is contained therein that those who have granted the imprimatur agree with the contents, opinions, or statements expressed.

The Illuminated Rosary, Revised Edition
The Luminous Mysteries
An Illustrated Rosary Book for Kids and Their Families

24 23 22 21 20 19   2 3 4 5 6 7 8 9

ISBN: 978-1-68192-511-0 (Inventory No. T2400)
LCCN: 2019939984

Book design and build by Steve Nagel.
Acknowledgments assistance by Sara Dethloff.
Proofing by Karen Carter.

See art credits, page 90, for copyright statements pertaining to individual artworks.

Our Sunday Visitor Publishing
www.osv.com